Woven Blessings: Poems of Identity, Faith, and Motherhood

Cammie Robinson

BookLeaf Publishing

India | USA | UK

Woven Blessings: Poems of Identity, Faith, and Motherhood © 2024 Cammie Robinson

Presentation by *BookLeaf Publishing*

Web: www.bookleafpub.com

E-mail: info@bookleafpub.com

ISBN: 9789360948405

First edition 2024

I dedicate this book to my husband and children, and also my therapists, who have helped me get through the challenges of my life. I also dedicate it to the ones who find themselves lost while trying to navigate their way through their own trauma and life's journey.

ACKNOWLEDGEMENT

I'm thankful to God for giving me the life I have, despite the intense amount of trauma and depression I've battled in my life. He sustains me and helps me through the hard times and reminds me that His love is sufficient.

PREFACE

I find solace and strength in weaving words that reflect the tapestry of my life. This preface serves as a heartfelt introduction to the verses that follow, providing a glimpse into the threads of identity, faith, and motherhood that have intricately shaped my journey.

These poems emerge from the depths of personal triumphs and challenges. As a Christian woman who has conquered the battle against obesity, as well as childhood abuse that lasted into early adulthood, I embark on a poetic exploration of the complexities surrounding adoption, past trauma, and the ongoing navigation of generational curses. Each verse is a reflection of my resilience, faith, and the profound experiences of being a wife and mother while also navigating my career in Child Welfare.

In sharing these poems, I hope to connect with readers on a profound level. Through the art of poetry, I aim to convey the beauty found in healing, the grace that sustains us through trials, and the strength discovered in the woven blessings of life's intricate design. As you delve into these pages, may you find echoes of your own journey, resonating with the universal themes that bind us together in the shared tapestry of humanity.

A Melody of Self-Love

On the playground's chaos, I stood alone,
Seeking validation, in a world unknown.
Anxious whispers, in voices prone,
To mock and jeer, my heart's gentle tone.

Desperate for attention, I'd make a scene,
Obnoxious antics, to fill the unseen.
Aching for acceptance, in the in-between,
Yearning for love, where hate had been.

Bullied and scorned, for all to see,
An outcast's fate, my reality.
Yet in my actions, a plea to be free,
From the shackles of insecurity.

In the laughter of others, I sought my worth,
Unaware of the pain, hidden beneath mirth.
But in the depths of loneliness, a rebirth,
A journey inward, to find my own berth.

In the shadow of rejection's bitter sting,
I found strength, a hidden gem within.
Embracing imperfections, I began to sing,
A melody of self-love, where new beginnings
spring.

A Lonely Puzzle Piece

Amidst the family portrait, I stood apart,
An unfamiliar face, a distant heart.
A puzzle piece misplaced, a lonely part,
In a world where belonging seemed to depart.

A stranger amidst kin, a foreign sight,
Inherited traits, a mismatched plight.
Invisible whispers, in shadows of night,
Felt like a burden, a constant fight.

Their laughter echoed, but I stood apart,
A melody foreign to my broken heart.
Unspoken words, tearing me apart,
In the realm of belonging, I played no part.

I watched from afar, longing to belong,
But my essence clashed, like a discordant song.
Unwanted echoes, where I didn't belong,
In the tapestry of family, I felt wronged.

A bothersome presence, an unwelcome guest,
A puzzle piece misplaced, put to the test.
In their eyes, I couldn't find rest,
An outcast's fate, by life's behest.

But amidst the darkness, a light did shine,
A journey inward, a soul to refine.
Finding solace in the depths of mine,
In self-acceptance, a truth divine.

For though I may not fit their mold,
My uniqueness is a story, waiting to unfold.
In the tapestry of life, my colors bold,
A belonging found, in self behold.

Hidden Origins

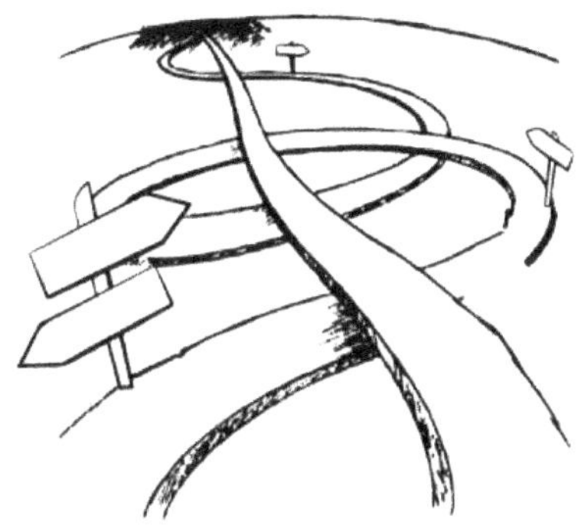

Within my family's embrace, shadows cast,
Alone I stood, a solitary contrast.
A puzzle piece astray, out of its past,
Unaware of the secret it amassed.

In the echoes of whispers, I heard the truth,
A revelation shattering my youth.
Adoption's secret, a heavy sleuth,
Unveiling the roots of my uncouth.

Unrelated by blood, a different kin,
Explaining the discord, the silence within.
Mismatched traits, where do I begin?
In the realm of belonging, I couldn't win.

Their laughter now tainted, a bittersweet,
As I grappled with the truth, incomplete.
A stranger among them, a silent beat,
In a family's tale, my seat deplete.

But in the revelation, a chasm grew wide,
A fracture in the family's pride.
No solace found in the truth belied,
As the sense of belonging continued to hide.

For though I may not share their name,
The truth of my origins, a lingering flame.
A void unfulfilled, a sense of shame,
In the shadow of adoption's claim.

Fostering Healing Light

At seventeen, a truth unveiled,
Adoption's tale, a ship set sailed.
Strained ties with adoptive parents, a turbulent
sea,
A storm of emotions, a soul not free.

Choices made, a tangled vine,
Through twists and turns, a troubled line.
Trauma's echo, a haunting score,
Yet resilience bloomed, like never before.

In the realm of child welfare, I found my way,
A path of healing, a brighter day.
Helping others, a purpose clear,
Fostering connections, banishing fear.

Career growth, a beacon light,
I faced my past, embraced the fight.
In healthy choices, redemption's key,
Transforming pain to legacy.

Through the verses of my life's design,
A tale of struggle, yet resilience shines.
In helping children, families find,
Permanency's embrace, a healing bind.

Rewritten Legacy: Pain to Purpose

In shadows cast by a father's hand,
A tale of pain, a life unplanned.
The echo of anger, a silent scream,
A haunting past, a fractured dream.

Through therapy, God's grace, and prayers
devout,
I faced the darkness and sought a way out.
A journey in Child Welfare, skills acquired and
refined,
To teach my father, get his emotions aligned.

Self-regulation is a delicate art,
Transforming rage to a brand-new start.
In the crucible of healing's flame,
Redemption whispers, a different name.

By God's grace, a guiding light,
Transformative moments lead to an end to the
night.
Grandkids embraced with love, not fear,
A legacy rewritten, the past made clear.

In the dance of time, a healing dance,
A second chance, a newfound stance.
From pain to purpose, a story unfolds,
A narrative rewritten, a bright future holds.

Generational Wounds

Amid the whispers of the past, shadows loom,
Generational wounds, a haunting gloom.
Yet in forgiveness' depths, hands find room,
A healing journey, hearts no longer consumed.

Forgiveness, a balm for wounds unseen,
A path to freedom, where scars convene.
In the tapestry of faith, a sacred sheen,
A journey of healing, where love redeems.

Through the lens of motherhood, we find,
A legacy of pain, left behind.
But in the embrace of love divine,
We break free from the chains that bind.

Forgiving ourselves, forgiving those who came before,
A journey of grace, where hearts restore.
In the light of forgiveness, we find the door,
To healing, to wholeness, forevermore.

For in forgiveness' embrace, we find release,
From the burdens of pain, a newfound peace.
In the journey of healing, our souls find ease,
As we embrace forgiveness, our hearts increase.

Woven Resilience

When facing trials, we must stand tall,
Resilience woven within our soul's thrall.
Through generations, it's passed, a call,
To rise above, to break down walls.

Like sturdy oaks in a tempest's rage,
Roots anchored deep, through every stage.
Though storms may come, we turn the page,
For in resilience, we find our gauge.

From parent to child, a legacy traced,
In the lines of strength, deeply embraced.
Through hardships endured, and battles faced,
Resilience blooms, a flower graced.

In the crucible of faith, resilience found,
A beacon of hope, on solid ground.
Through valleys low, and mountains crowned,
Resilience guides, where love is bound.

So let us stand, in resilience's might,
In the darkest hour, we shine bright.
For in the journey of faith and flight,
Resilience leads us to the light.

Therapeutic Embrace

Among the shadows of my past,
A journey unfolds, slow but steadfast.
Forced into therapy's grasp at seventeen,
A bitter pill, a reluctant routine.

Discovering truths through digital streams,
The revelation of adoption's seams.
A wound reopened, a shattered dream,
Unraveling the fabric of my esteem.

At first, I resisted, closed and withdrawn,
Afraid to confront the pain head-on.
Yet as the years passed, maturity dawned,
And I found the courage to journey on.

Mid-twenties brought a newfound resolve,
To face the demons, to problems solve.
Therapy's embrace, a mystery to solve,
A beacon of hope in the darkness, to evolve.

Through gentle guidance and empathetic ear,
I learned to confront what I once feared.
To navigate trauma, to persevere,
And shed the weight of yesteryear.

Therapy became a sanctuary, a place to explore,
The depths of my soul, the wounds I bore.
With coping skills in hand, I could soar,
Towards a future where healing is in store.

No longer shackled by the past's cruel decree,
I forge ahead, stronger, resilient, free.
For therapy's gift is the clarity to see,
That growth and healing begin with me.

Gone

Those were the days that I hated being me
Those were the days that I felt I wasn't free
Those were the days that I cried all night long
Those were the days where I felt I didn't belong.

I would look in the mirror and think "why are
these people so mean?"
Was it just me? Or was it something unseen?
People liked to say "yeah, she's okay, she has a
cute face"
They said it as if being full-figured is such a
disgrace.

They were always saying to me that I'm
unhealthy and I'm fat;
but what gets me is they said it to my face actin'
like I didn't already know that.
You don't think I couldn't see? Clearly I'm not
blind;
but the way that I look is NOT how I'm defined.

It's crazy how people treat you so differently
when you don't fit into their definition of pretty
It's like if you're not itty-bitty you can't even be
a part of their committee.
But I refuse to be a victim to the stereotyping
and judging
because I know by God's grace I was born to be
something.
It took me forever to understand it's not about
how others feel.
It's about how God created to be someone real.

I'm beautiful, vibrant and above all, I'm smart;
and there's more to me than my weight cause I
also have a big heart.
So, damn right I have a cute face, hell yeah I
sure am thick in the waist;
but listen when I say, I look good whether I'm
wearing cotton, denim, leather, and even lace.

As I grew up I took the time to learn about the
strength of my body.
Simply thinking back to the days when I was in
Karate.
Focusing on sparring, my form, and even my
posture
it was then I knew my bad habits had to make
their departure.

One and a half years later and 125 pounds down
People often looked at me like I was a new girl
in town.
New people that I'd meet couldn't believe I was
ever large;
So I'd show them my loose skin and told them
for my health I took charge.

Through perseverance and learning how to truly
love myself,
I'm now the best version of me, not the best
version of someone else.

So gone are the days that I hated being me
Gone are the days that I felt I wasn't free
Gone are the days that I cried all night long
Because today is the day where I know I belong.

The Mind's Turmoil

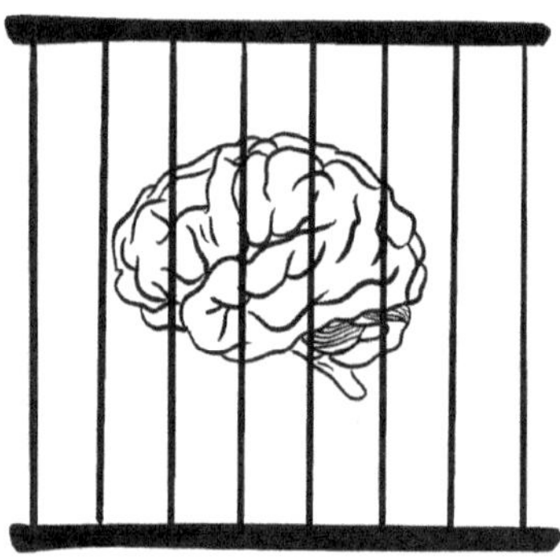

Within the chaos of a thousand thoughts,
A mind in turmoil, a battle fought.
Each moment a whirlwind, a tempest wrought,
ADHD's grip, relentless and taut.

From classroom woes to life's disarray,
Focus eludes, slips away.
Math and reading, day by day,
Remediation's shadow, in dismay.

Dreams of art, and other classes delight,
But trapped in the maze of academic plight.
A mind adrift, lost in flight,
Struggling to find the path that's right.

Clean and organized, the desired state,
But clutter and chaos, a constant trait.
In a world of disorder, I navigate,
Seeking solace, in a cluttered fate.

Medication forgotten, lost in the fray,
A fleeting thought, fades away.
In the labyrinth of each passing day,
ADHD's burden, here to stay.

Yet amidst the struggle, a glimmer shines,
A journey of coping, amidst the confines.
Seeking solutions, through the confines,
Finding strength, in the chaos' binds.

Glistening Vulnerability

I see the depths of darkness, where shadows reign,
A battle rages, an unrelenting pain.
Depression's grip, a heavy chain,
Anxiety's whispers, a relentless strain.

But amidst the storm, a flicker of light,
A glimmer of hope, shining bright.
With each step forward, we take flight,
Towards the dawn, where fears take flight.

Through tear-stained nights and weary days,
We navigate the labyrinth, in myriad ways.
Seeking solace, in the sun's warm rays,
In the journey of healing, where hearts ablaze.

With each breath taken, a new beginning,
In the embrace of love, our souls singing.
Finding strength in vulnerability's glistening,
As we rise from the ashes, resilience bringing.

For in the depths of despair, we find,
A strength within, of a different kind.
A resilience forged, in the crucible of mind,
A testament to the human spirit, refined.

Navigating Shadows

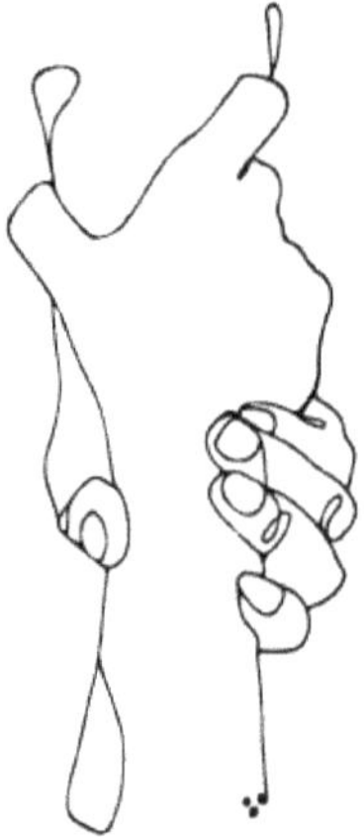

Deep in my trenches of trauma, I stand,
A beacon of hope in a troubled land.
Working with children, hand in hand,
Navigating shadows, where scars expand.

Their stories unfold, in whispers and cries,
Reflections of pain, hidden behind their eyes.
As I hold their hands, my heart sighs,
Knowing the road ahead, where healing lies.

But in the depths of their trauma's grasp,
I confront my own demons, an arduous task.
Unraveling memories, an emotional mask,
In the shadows of trauma, I dare not bask.

Through therapy's embrace, I learn to cope,
Navigating the labyrinth of pain's scope.
Developing resilience, in a world of nope,
For the children's sake, I find new hope.

In their laughter, I find solace and grace,
A balm for wounds, a sacred space.
In helping them heal, I find my place,
In the journey of trauma, we both embrace.

A Dance of Tasks

With the hustle and bustle of the day's demand,
A list of tasks, like grains of sand.
To prioritize, a skill so grand,
In the journey of productivity, where we stand.

First, assess the urgency, the time at hand,
Identify deadlines, like a guiding strand.
Breaking tasks into smaller, manageable bands,
Allows for focus, where clarity expands.

Next, consider importance, like a command,
Distinguish the vital from the unplanned.
Prioritize goals, with a steadfast brand,
To steer towards success, as dreams are fanned.

Delegate when possible, to share the load,
Empower others, where talents are sowed.
And don't forget self-care, along the road,
For a balanced life, is the ultimate code.

In the dance of tasks, find harmony's key,
Balance urgency with importance, set free.
With clarity and focus, let priorities decree,
A path to success, where we aim to be.

Divine Awakening

In the midst of darkness, at twenty years old,
Lost in the chaos, my story untold.
Bad choices consumed me, my spirit cold,
Until a whisper of grace, a hand to hold.

Drawn to the light by voices sincere,
Six months of persuasion, their plea I'd hear.
To church I relented, to quell their cheer,
But little did I know, God was near.

In the quiet of the sanctuary's embrace,
I felt His presence, a sacred grace.
A voice within, in my own space,
Whispered softly, a divine embrace.

"I have your back," the words resound,
Echoes of love, profound and profound.
In that moment, clarity found,
As God's hand reached, my heart unbound.

Tears of redemption, a soul reborn,
In the arms of grace, all burdens shorn.
For the path ahead, no longer worn,
With God by my side, a new dawn sworn.

Inviting Him in, the most important choice,
Heeding His voice, my inner voice.
In His love, I found my voice,
In His presence, I rejoice.

Lifting Burdens, Seeking Grace

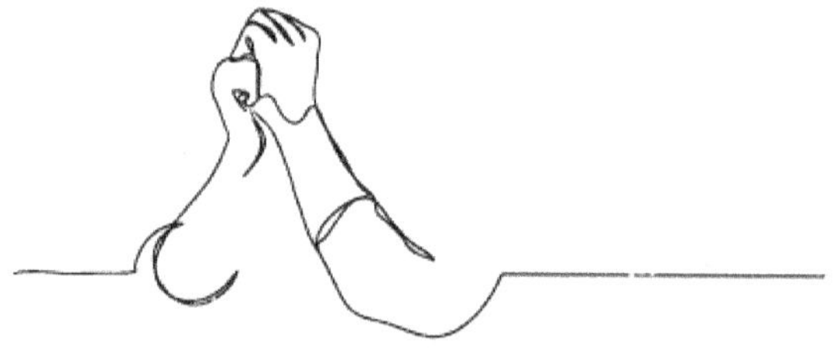

With the quiet of dawn, I bow my head,
Praying for the children, their futures ahead.
In the stillness of night, where dreams are fed,
I lift up their names, where hope is spread.

For the foster children, with hearts so tender,
Navigating life's storms, in a world so splintered.
May they find solace, in arms surrendered,
Guided by love, in moments untethered.

For the biological families, in shadows cast,
Bearing burdens heavy, memories vast.
May they find redemption, in futures amassed,
Healing old wounds, breaking free at last.

In the quiet whispers of prayer's embrace,
I lift their burdens, seeking grace.
For in love's shelter, they find their place,
In the sacred journey, where hearts find space.

Paths Intertwined

Within the loud halls of our church, we met,
A hug exchanged, no regrets to fret.
Months passed, friendship bloomed, yet,
Only in group settings, our connection set.

Years drifted by, our paths intertwined,
Occasional meetups, our friendship defined.
Till one day, a message, fate aligned,
A conversation sparked, hearts entwined.

Nervousness tingled on our first date's eve,
Anxiety whispered, will he perceive?
But as we talked, doubts did leave,
In his presence, I began to believe.

A kiss beneath the stars, our bond did seal,
Emotions deepened, love's gentle appeal.
In his arms, I found solace and zeal,
Protected and cherished, in love's surreal.

In the journey of love, we embarked anew,
Each moment together, our bond grew.
Through laughter and tears, trials we'd rue,
Yet hand in hand, we'd see it through.

Nervousness melted to comfort's embrace,
In his eyes, I found my sacred space.
A love so tender, a gentle grace,
In his arms, I found my rightful place.

Through the seasons, our love would bloom,
In sunshine and rain, dispelling gloom.
Building dreams, banishing the gloom,
Together, our hearts would always resume.

In his embrace, I found my shelter,
His love, a flame that couldn't falter.
In his arms, I found my better,
Our love, a bond no one could sever.

So here we stand, side by side,
In love's embrace, our hearts abide.
Together, in life's endless ride,
With him, my love, forever allied.

A Mother's Guilt

As I listen to all the whispers of the night,
I never dreamed of motherhood's light.
But fate had plans beyond my sight,
And with you, love, everything felt right.

On our wedding night, a seed was sown,
A life within us, suddenly grown.
I grappled with fears, felt so alone,
Yet his presence, my heart had known.

When he arrived, a bundle of joy,
I felt emotions I couldn't deploy.
Baby blues clouded, my heart would toy,
With guilt and tears, I couldn't destroy.

Unable to nurse, my body's decree,
The weight of inadequacy instantly crushed me.
I cried silent tears, no solace to see,
Lost in a storm, longing to be free.

My husband stood by, his love so true,
But how could he help when I scarcely knew?
Wrapped in a fog, emotions askew,
I searched for a light to guide me through.

Slowly, I learned to let go of the guilt,
To cherish the moments, the love we built.
For a child fed, whether breast or bottle spilt,
Is nourished by love, not milk's quilt.

In time, I found peace in motherhood's embrace,
Accepting imperfection with beauty and grace.
For in his eyes, I see love's trace,
And in his smile, my heart finds its place.

So here I stand, a mother strong and true,
With scars and tears, but love renewed.
In his laughter, my soul finds its cue,
To embrace each moment, with gratitude.

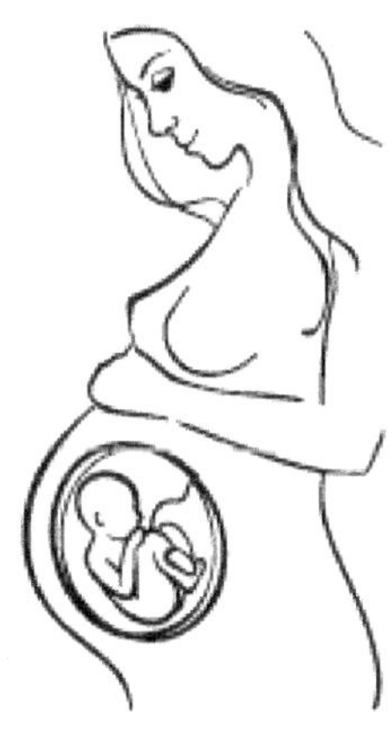

Resounding Echoes

In the echoes of my past, I find
The heavyweight of generational bind.
A legacy of trauma, deeply entwined,
Leaving scars on the soul, the heart, the mind.

Raised in the shadow of anger's blaze,
Where discipline was met with harsh displays.
My father's voice, a thunderous craze,
Instilling fear in my childhood days.

I bear the weight of hidden scars,
Embedded deep within my heart's memoirs.
Yearning to break from anger's bars,
Its grip relentless, leaving jagged scars.

Now as a parent, I stand on the brink,
Facing the demons I've tried to unlink.
But the echoes of childhood, they still slink,
In moments of frustration, I'm on the brink.

My children, innocent and free,
Unknowing of the pain inside of me.
Yet when tantrums rage, I cannot see,
Beyond the shadows of what used to be.

Frustration boils, emotions rise,
As echoes of the past crystallize.
I yell, I scream, through tear-stained eyes,
Caught in the cycle, to my surprise.

But in the depths of my turmoil's thrum,
I find the strength to overcome.
To break the chains, to become numb,
To the echoes of anger, I succumb.

For in the eyes of my children dear,
I see the chance to make things clear.
To rewrite the script, to persevere,
And break the cycle of pain and fear.

So I'll learn to self-regulate,
To navigate emotions, love, and hate.
To heal the wounds of a broken state,
And forge a path to a brighter fate.

Sacred Struggles of Self-Forgiveness

At the break of dawn, as sunlight streams,
With three in tow, my morning dreams.
Roles in flux, like endless streams,
A balancing act, in life's extremes.

With apron strings tied, and briefcase in hand,
I navigate life's intricate strand.
Mother, wife, worker, all grand,
Yet beneath the surface, a silent demand.

In the church's embrace, I find solace anew,
Serving others, my heart rings true.
But in the shadows, a whispered cue,
To tend to my soul, to find what's due.

For in the endless cycle of giving,
A piece of myself, I find myself living.
Yet in the quiet moments, in stillness forgiving,
I reclaim my worth, in self-forgiving.

Learning to balance, to prioritize me,
Amidst the chaos, to find serenity.
For in nurturing myself, I truly see,
The strength to flourish, to live fully free.

Life's Mixing Bowl: Work, Life, and Parenting

In the morning's rush, the day's begun,
A parent's journey, work and children spun.
Balancing tasks, under the sun,
Parenting and career, intertwined as one.

From dawn's first light to the evening's call,
We navigate the hurdles, big and small.
With hearts divided, yet standing tall,
In the dance of parenthood, we give our all.

Work calls beckon, deadlines loom near,
But in our hearts, our children's cheer.
Their laughter, their smiles, ever dear,
Remind us of what truly matters here.

In the midst of meetings and emails sent,
We steal moments, time well spent.
With children's laughter, our spirits lent,
Finding joy in the midst of life's ascent.

Though the path is laden with obstacles in tow,
We persevere, our love aglow.
For in the balance of work and family's flow,
We find the strength to make it so.

So here's to the parents, the ones who strive,
To keep the flame of family alive.
In the balancing act, we learn to thrive,
In parenthood and career, side by side.

Reflective Journey

Within life's grand tome's final pages,
The end of our journey, through time's stages.
Through valleys low and sky's vast reaches,
We've journeyed far, to find what life teaches.

In the tapestry of words, both joy and pain,
We've woven threads, in sunshine and rain.
Each poem a chapter, a heartfelt refrain,
A testament to the human spirit's gain.

As we close this book, let us reflect,
On the lessons learned, on paths intersect.
In the beauty of life, let us detect,
The love that binds, the hearts connect.

For though the pages may come to a close,
Our story continues, where the river flows.
In the journey of life, where each moment
shows,
The beauty of existence, in highs and lows.

So let us carry these words within,
In the depths of our souls, where they begin.
For in the echoes of each poem's spin,
We find the essence of life, therein.
With gratitude and love, we turn the final page,
A journey shared, from youth to sage.
In the closing lines of life's grand stage,
We find peace and solace, in life's embrace.